YOU'RE THE V...
Dean Martin

	In the Book	On the CD
I Will	4	Track 1
Just In Time	8	Track 2
Kiss	14	Track 4
Let Me Go Lover	11	Track 3
Little Ole Wine Drinker Me	16	Track 5
Naughty Lady Of Shady Lane	22	Track 6
Rio Bravo	46	Track 10
Somewhere There's A Someone	28	Track 7
That's Amore	32	Track 8
Volare	40	Track 9

© International Music Publications Limited
Griffin House 161 Hammersmith Road London W6 8BS England

Editorial, arranging, engraving and recording Artemis Music Limited (www.artemismusic.com)
Design: IMP Studio
Photography: Bob Willoughby / Redferns Music Picture Library

Published 2004

© International Music Publications Limited
Griffin House 161 Hammersmith Road London W6 8BS England

 Reproducing this music in any form is illegal and forbidden by the Copyright, Designs and Patents Act 1988

Dean Martin
Born June 7th 1917
Died December 25th 1995

A true icon of the entertainment business if ever there was one, Dean Martin's beginnings were considerably less auspicious than the show biz life-style he was to experience during the 1950s and 60s heyday of film and TV.

Born Dino Paul Crocetti, the son of an immigrant barber, he only spoke Italian until the age of five. After school his first job was in the Ohio steel mills. He then became a croupier before renaming himself Dean Martini, setting out to become a crooner in the style of his idol Bing Crosby. Having dropped the last 'i' from his surname, Martin's early career was mostly unsuccessful until, in 1946, he meet Jerry Lewis and the two teamed up, eventually becoming star performers as a comedy act and in films. They headlined in the 1951 film *At War With The Army* and, in total, starred in 13 Paramount movies.

By 1956 however, the duo were hardly speaking to each other and Martin set out on a solo career. Apart from his 1953 hit *That's Amore*, he had not had great success as a singer, but in 1958 he reappeared on screen alongside Marlon Brando in *The Young Lions*. Then another hit song, *Volare*, ensured that he was now a regular face in movies, music, stage and TV.

His appearance with Frank Sinatra in the 1959 movie *Some Came Running*, led to the formation of the Rat Pack (most famously as a trio with Sammy Davis Jnr.), setting new standards of celebrity excess. Martin was unashamedly Sinatra's right-hand man, admitting "…we cut the top of our thumbs and became brothers."

In the late 1970s however, Martin's health began to fail and in 1987 he suffered the loss of his son Dean Paul in an air crash, a blow from which he never fully recovered. His frail state led to his withdrawal from a Rat Pack reunion tour in 1988 and, having spent his final years in virtual solitude, he died of respiratory failure on Christmas Morning in 1995.

"He's got a great sense of timing. He never presses." Jackie Gleason

I Will

Words and Music by Richard Glasser

Backing

Medium pop

I don't wan-na be the one to say I'm gon-na miss you, but I will.

I don't wan-na say I'm gon-na cry my eyes out ba-by, but I

© 1962 (renewed) Ridgeway Music Company Inc, USA
This arrangement © 2004 Ridgeway Music Company Inc, USA
All Rights Reserved. Used by permission.

Just In Time

Words by Betty Comden and Adolph Green
Music by Jule Styne

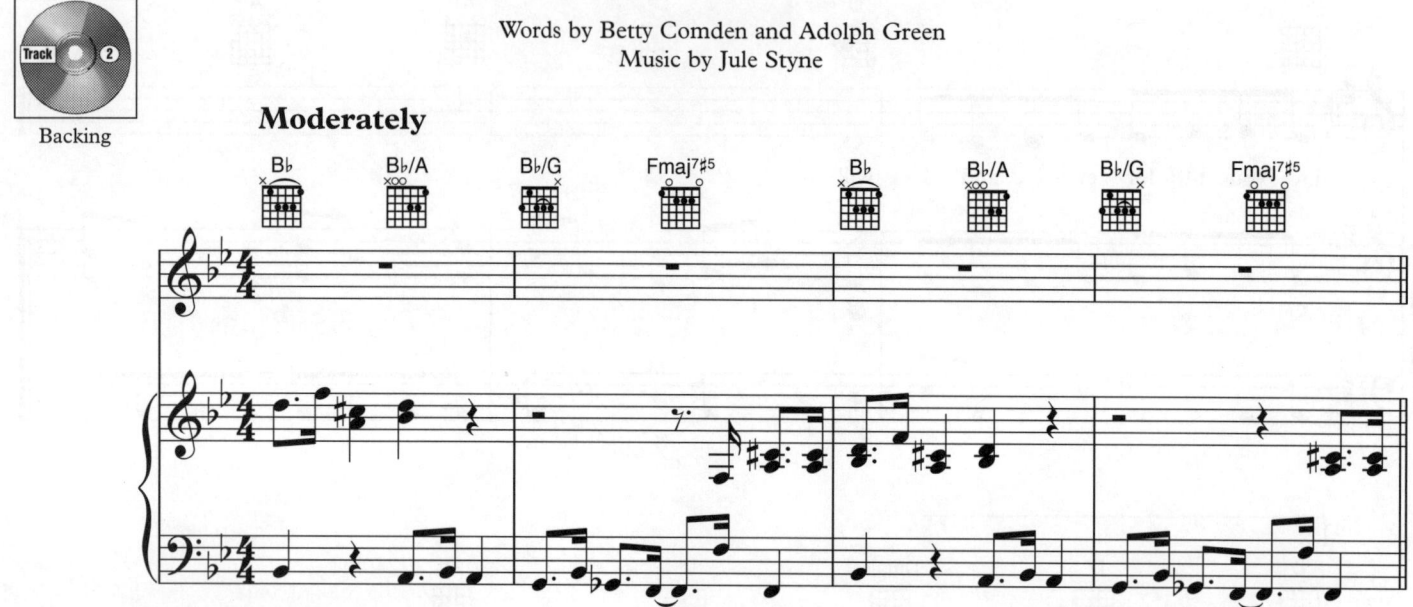

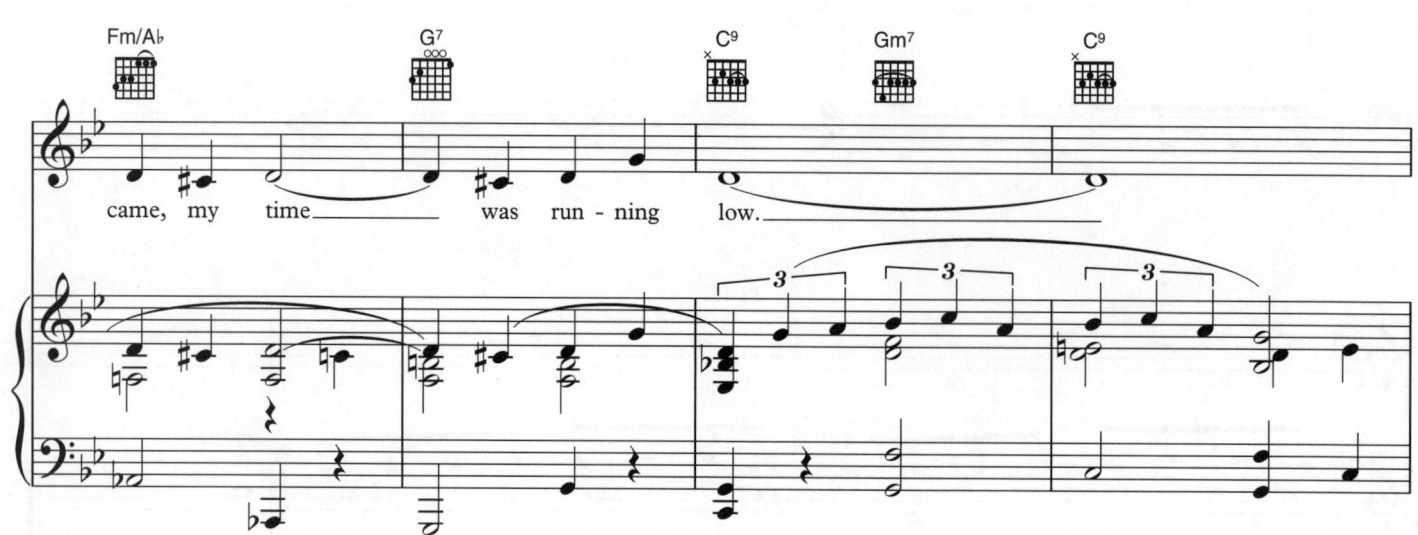

© 1956 (renewed) Stratford Music Corp, USA
Warner/Chappell North America Ltd, London W6 8BS

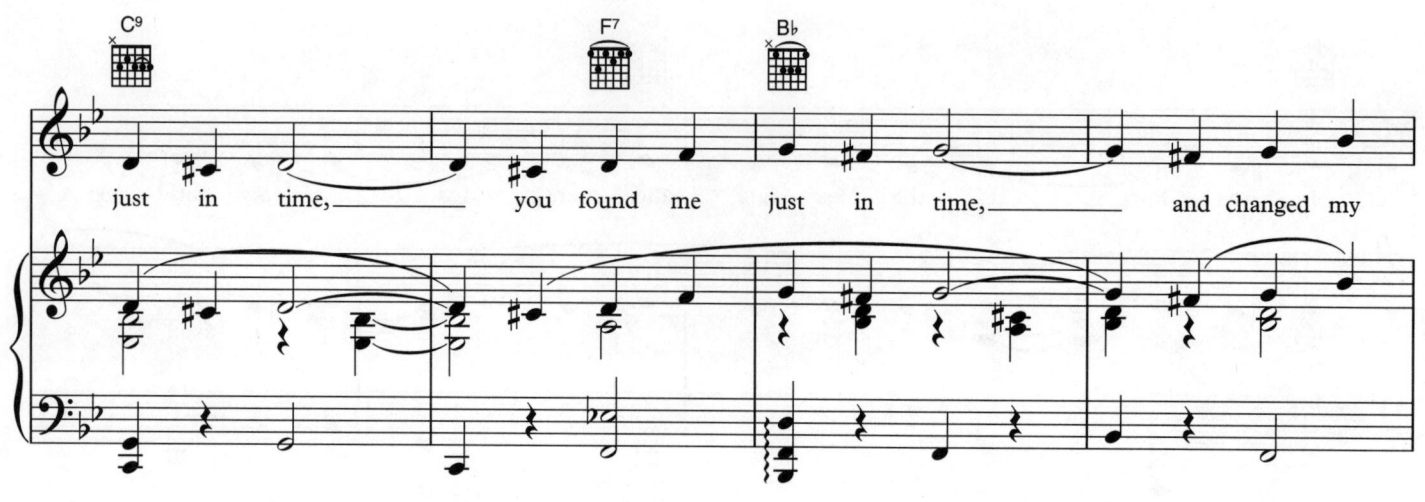
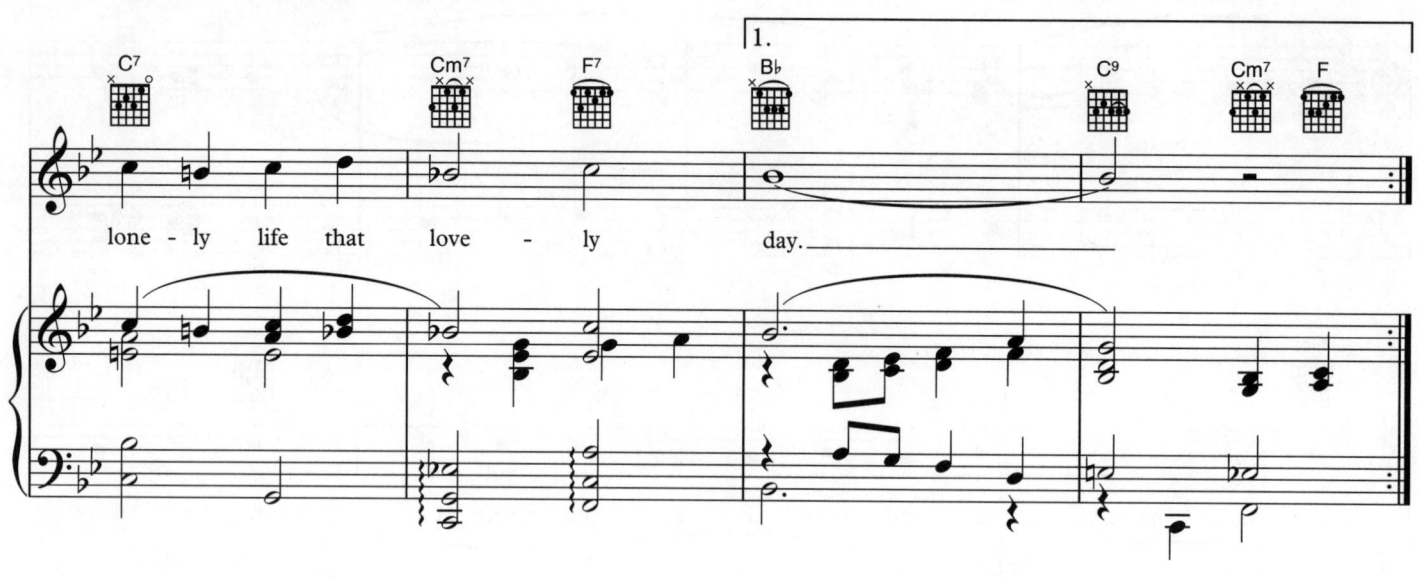
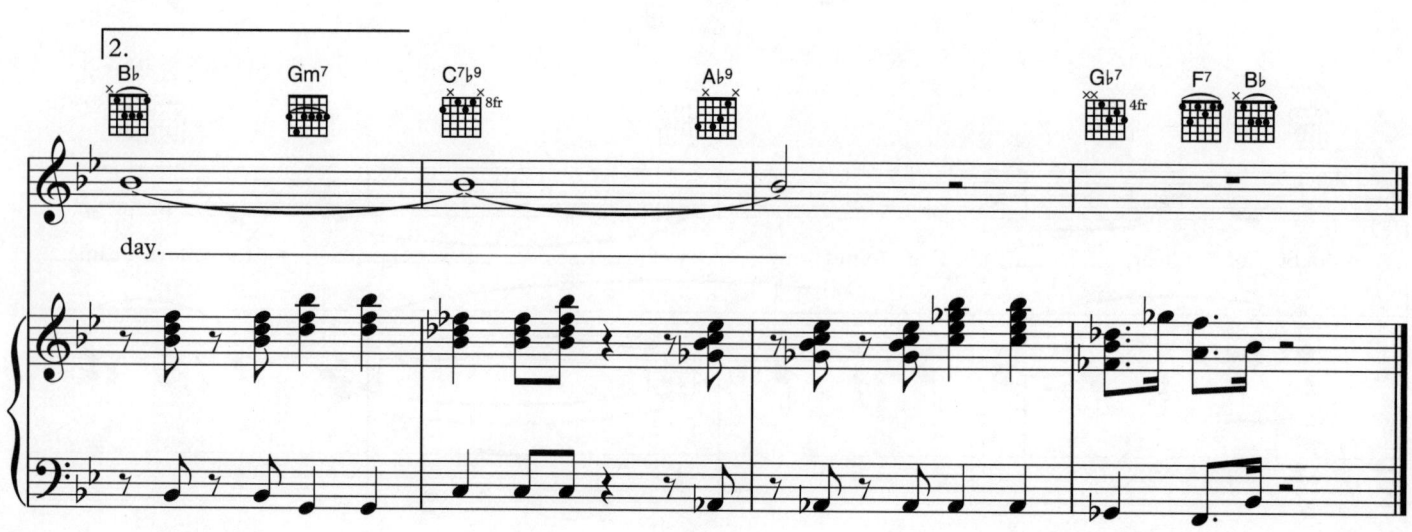

Let Me Go Lover

Words and Music by Jenny Carson

Backing

Slowly, with feeling

Oh let me go, let me go, let me go, lov-er. Let me be, set me free from your spell. You made me

© 1954 Hill And Range Songs Inc, USA
Carlin Music Corp, London NW1 8BD

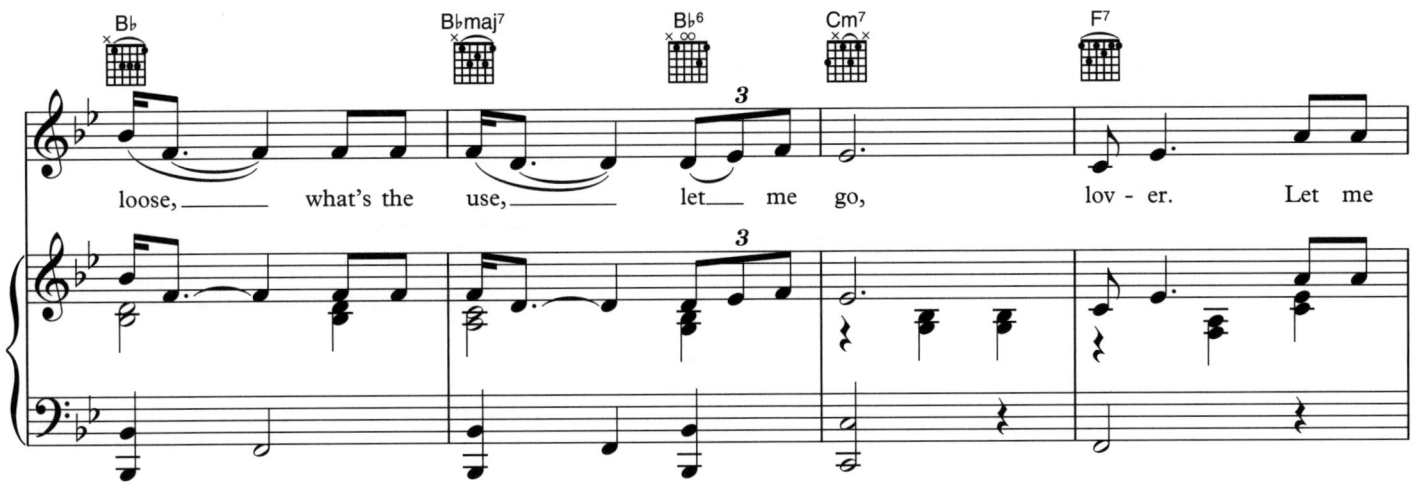
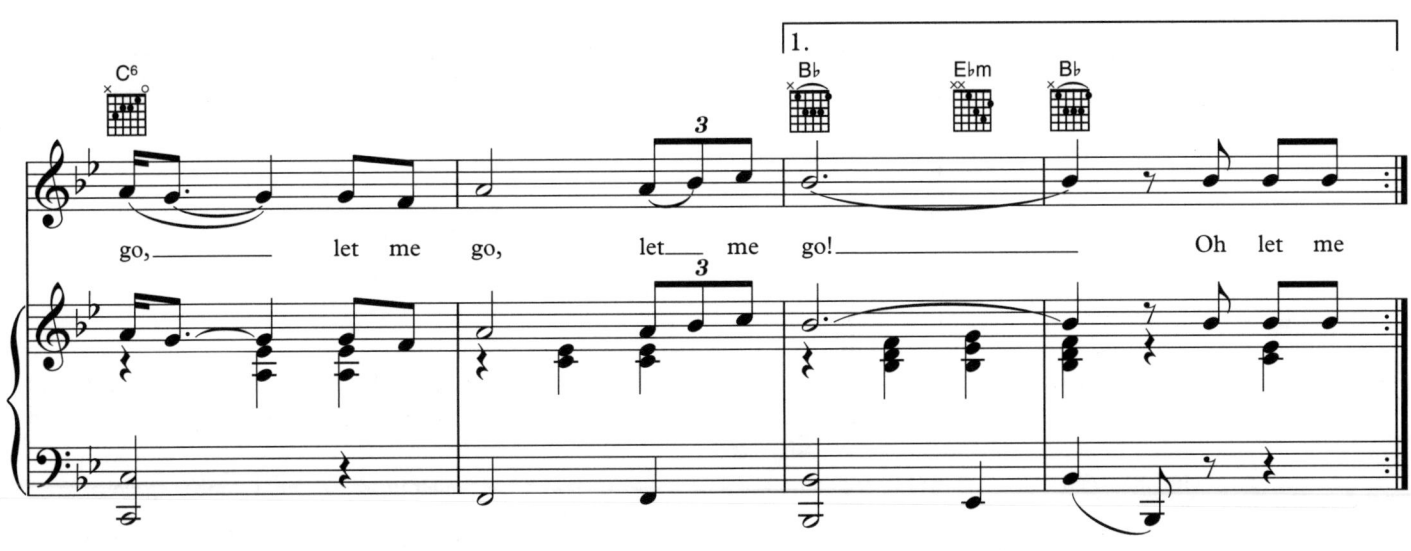

Little Ole Wine Drinker Me

Words and Music by Hank Mills and Dick Jennings

Backing

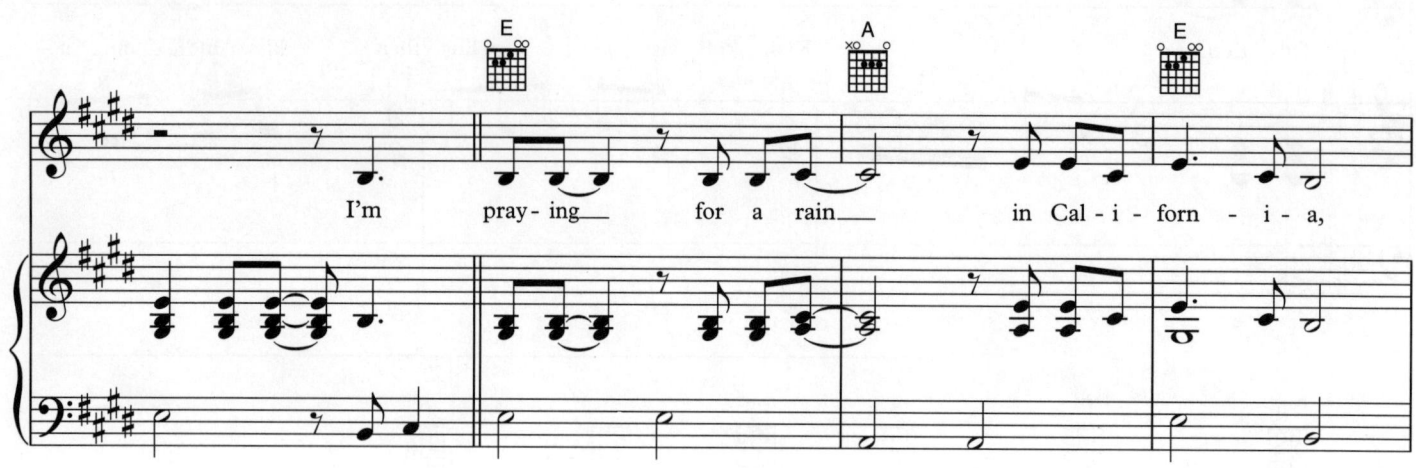

I'm pray-ing for a rain in Cal-i-forn-i-a,

so the grapes can grow and they can make more wine.

© 1966 Moss-Rose Publishing Inc, USA
Carlin Music Corp, London NW1 8BD

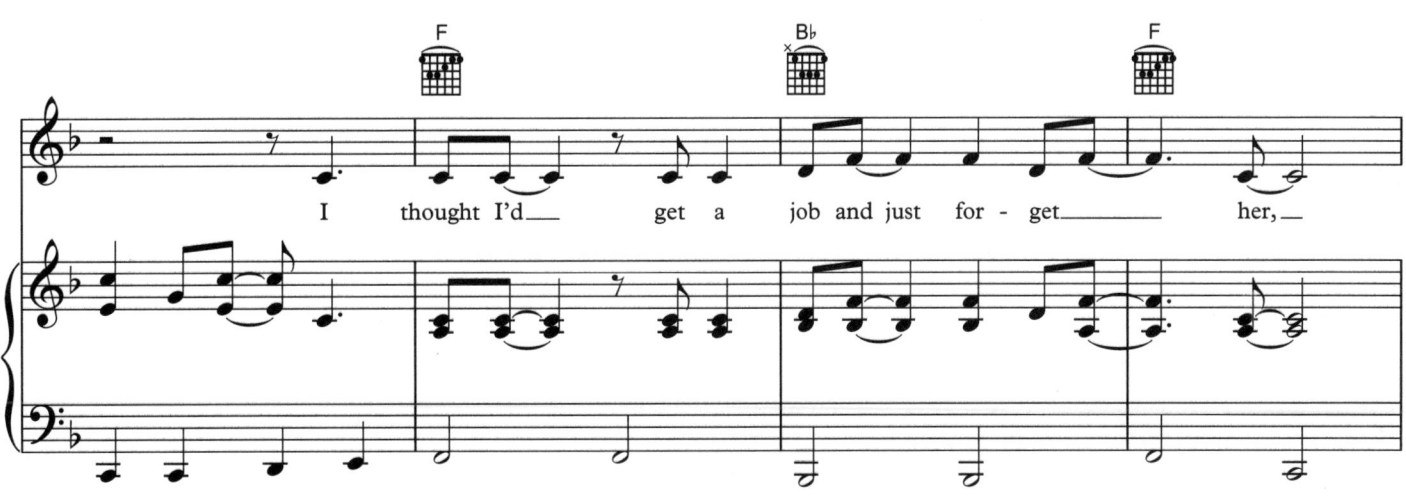
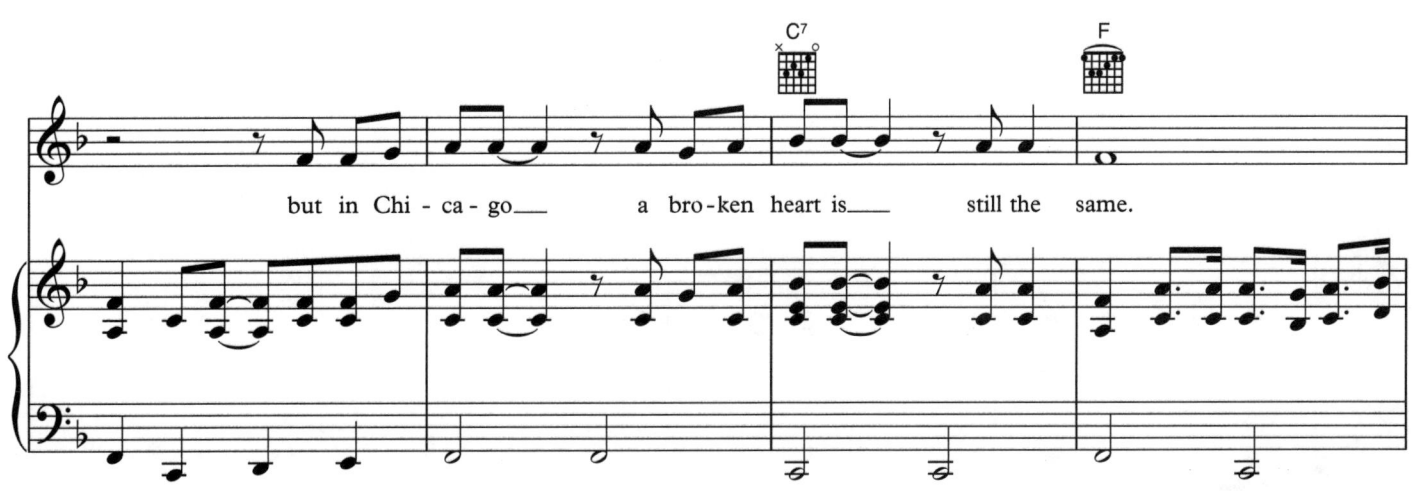

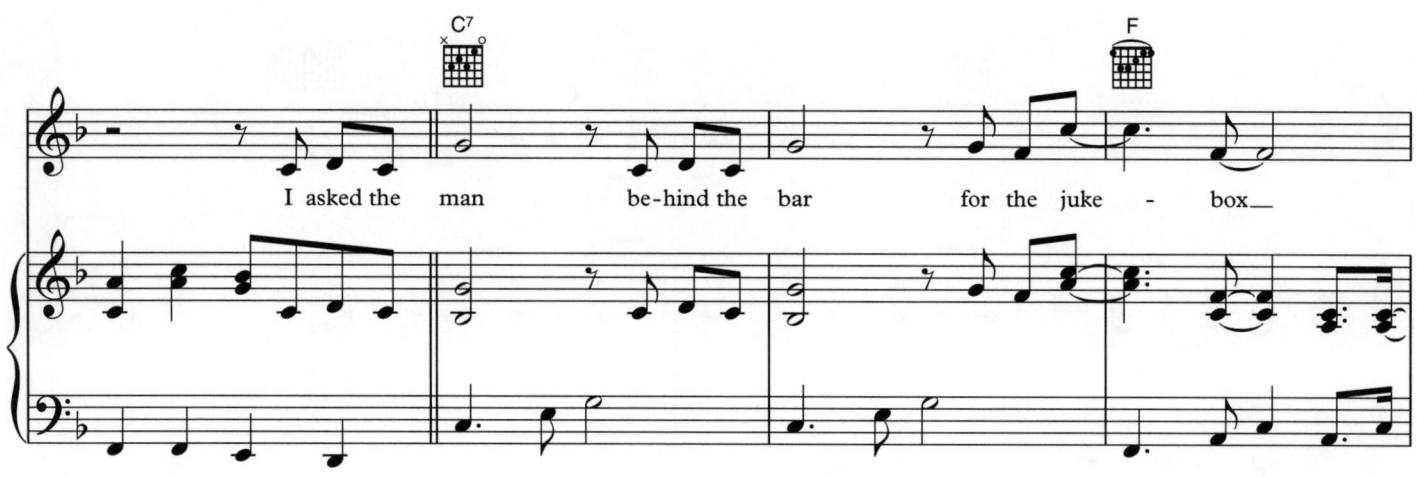

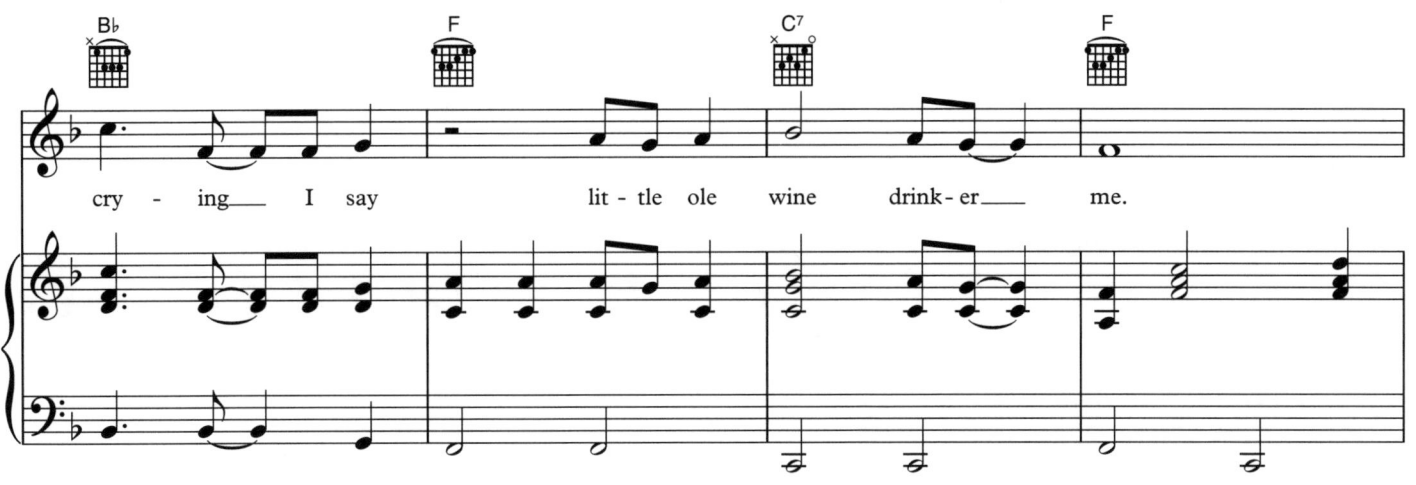
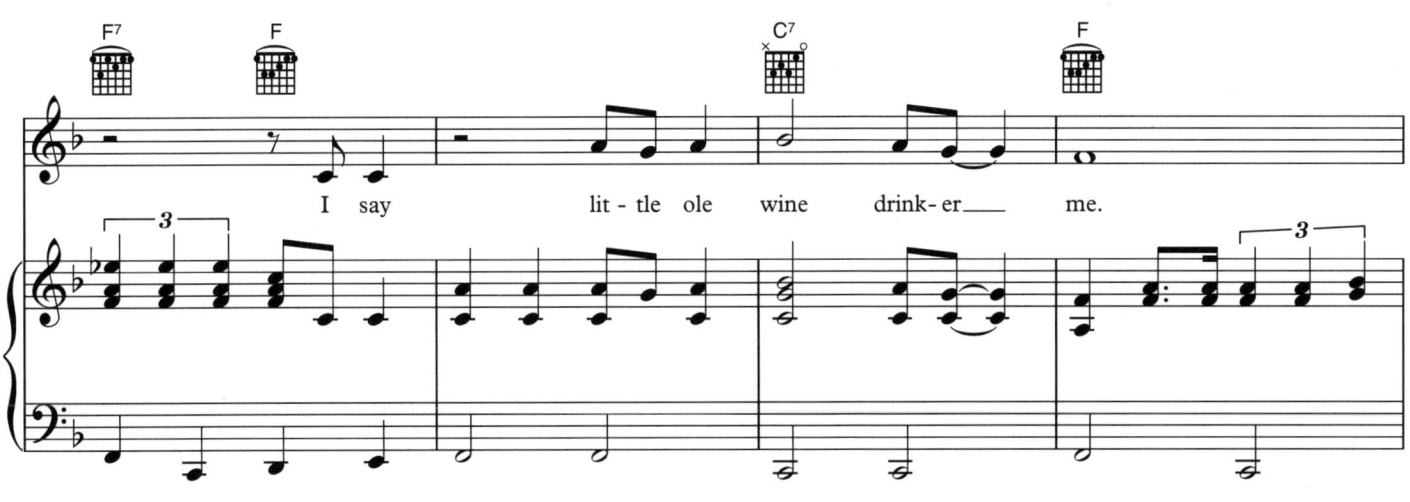

Naughty Lady Of Shady Lane

Words and Music by Roy Bennett and Sid Tepper

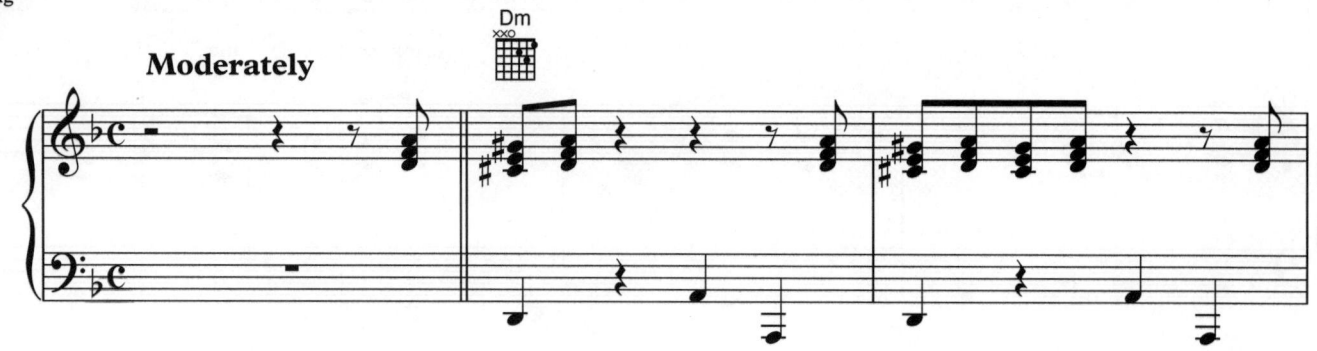

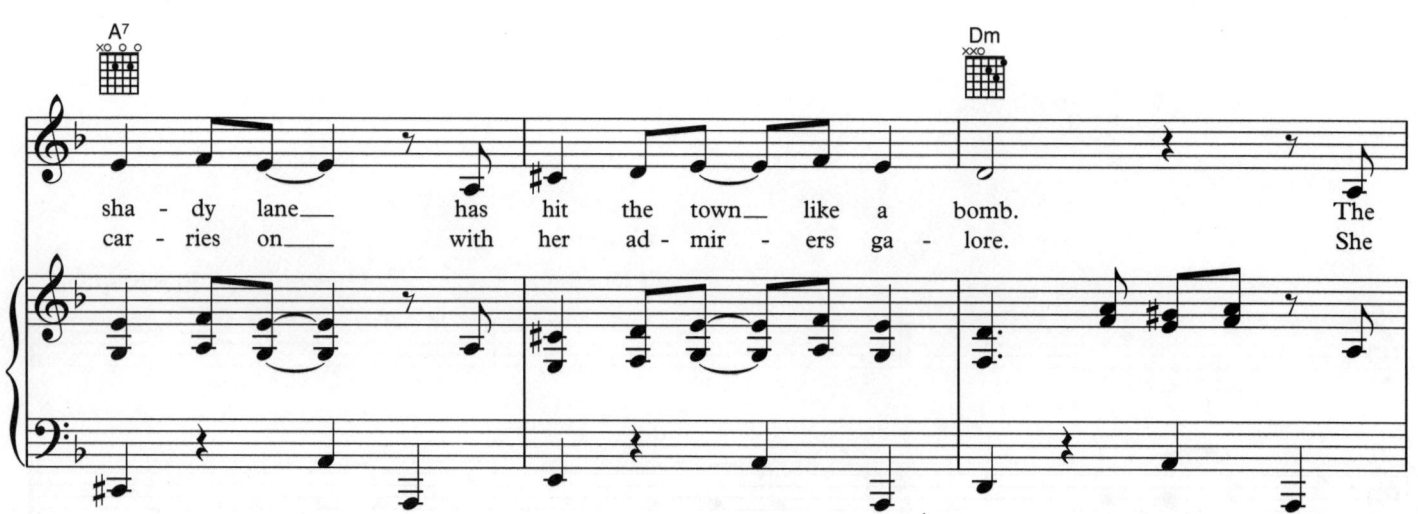

© 1961 George Paxton Inc, USA
Warner/Chappell North America Ltd, London W6 8BS

26

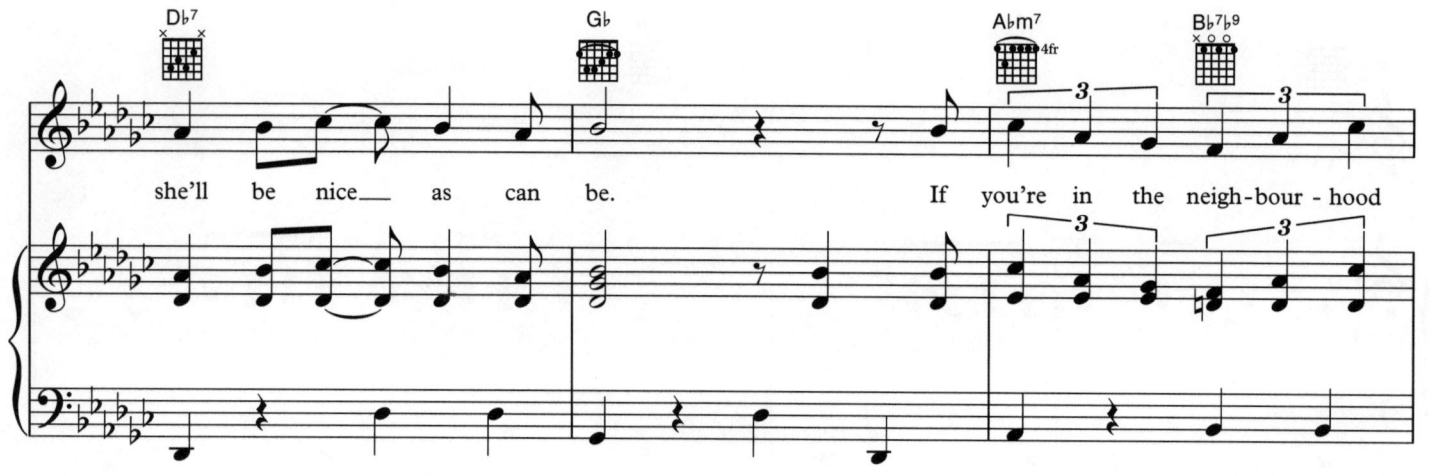

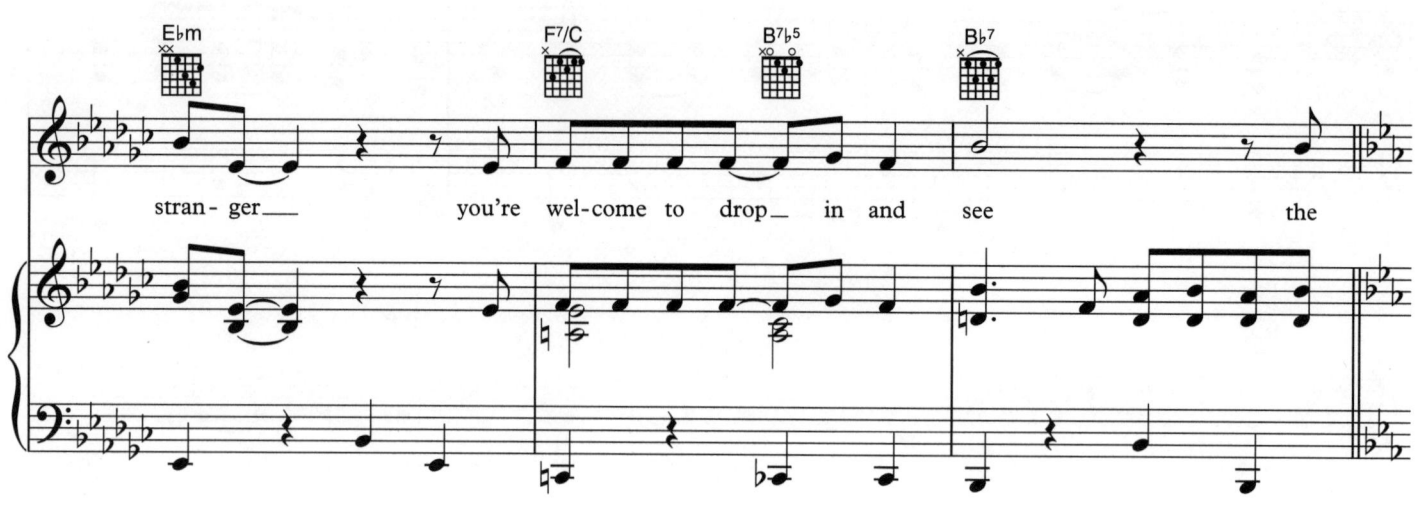

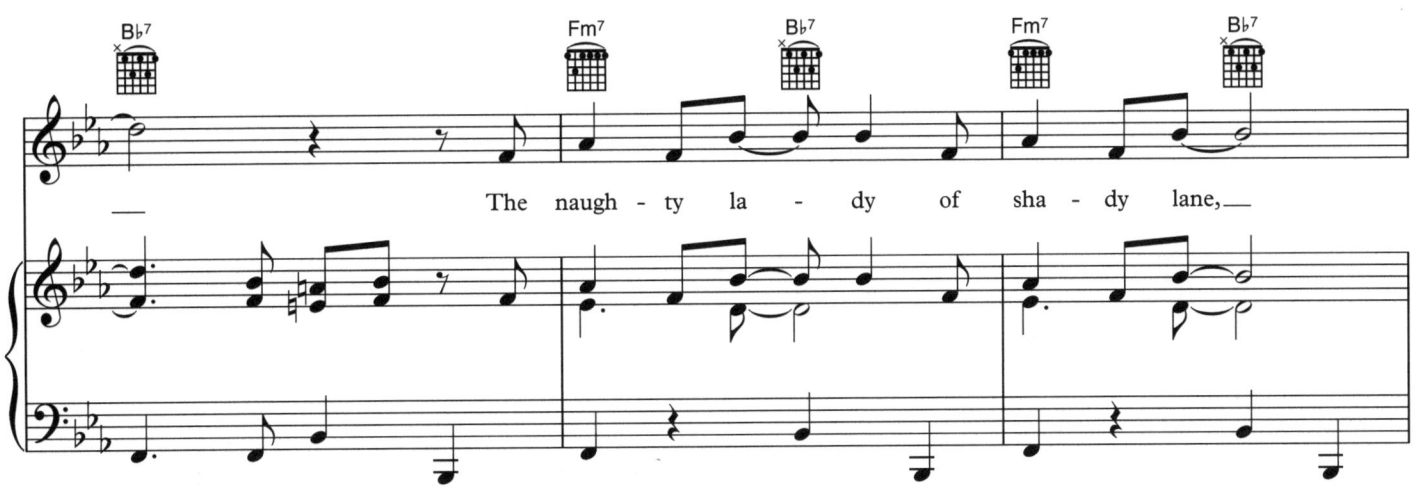

Somewhere There's A Someone

Words and Music by Baker Knight

Backing

Medium rock

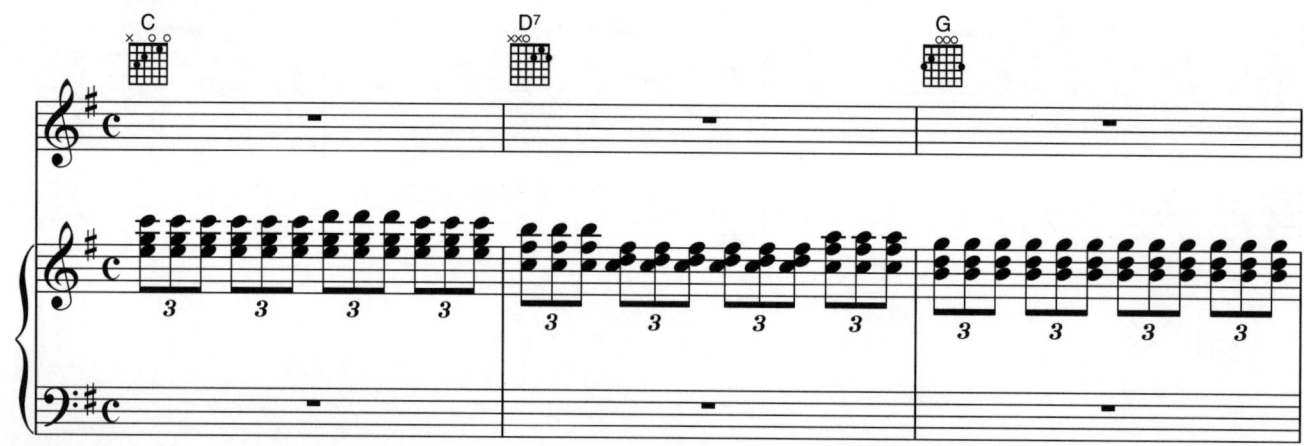

Some-where there's a some-one___ for

ev-'ry-one, some-where___ there's a

© 1966 (renewed) Noma-Music Inc, USA
Warner/Chappell North America Ltd, London W6 8BS

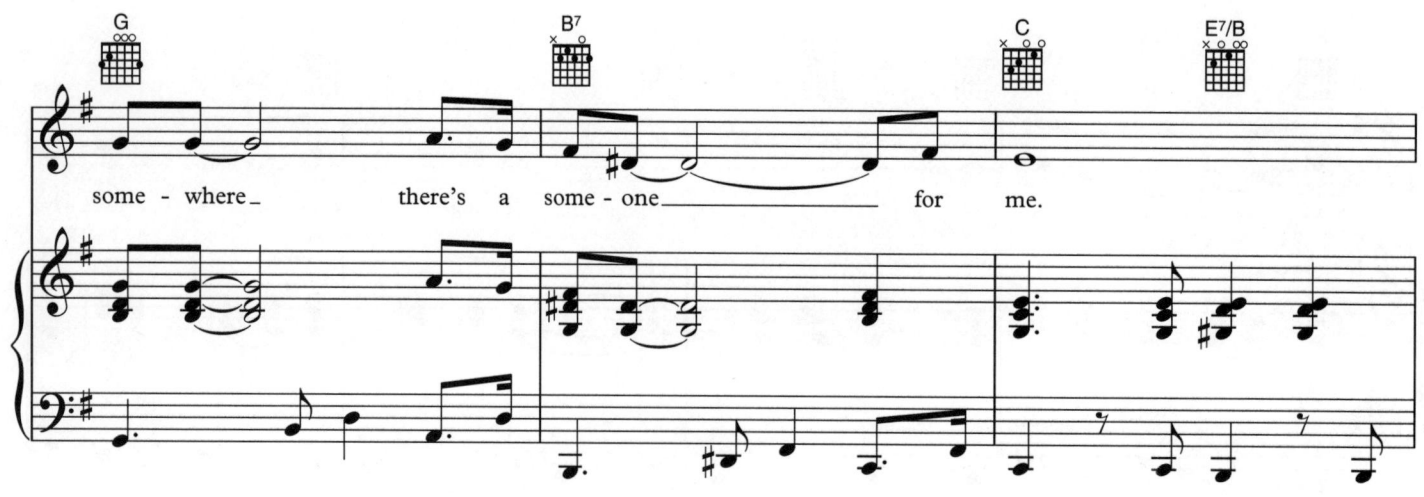
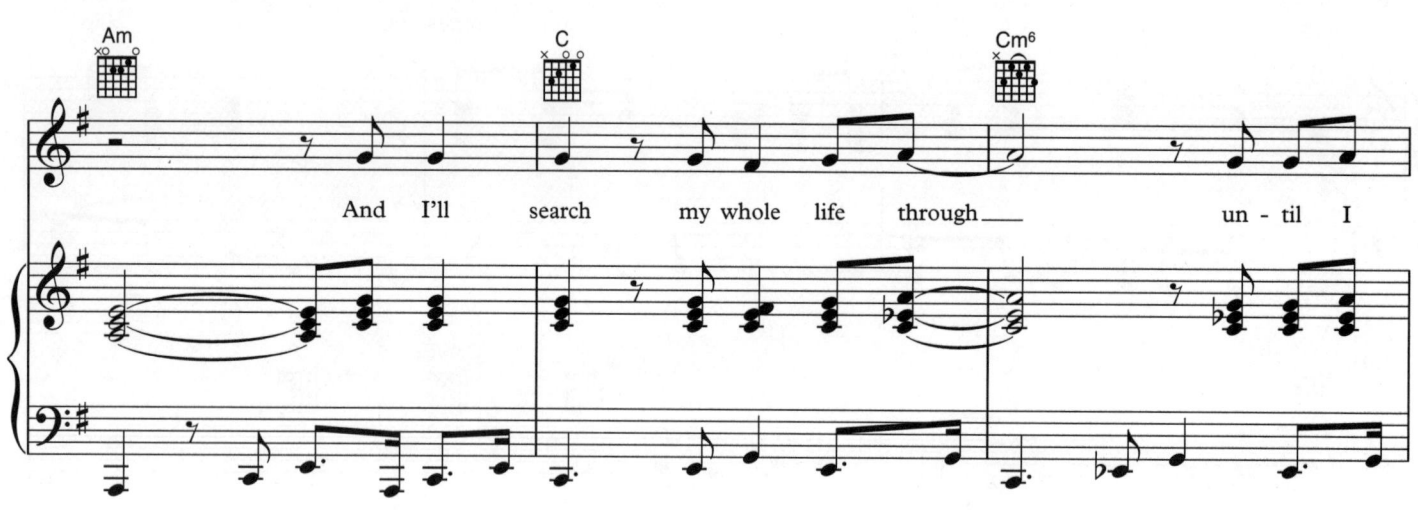
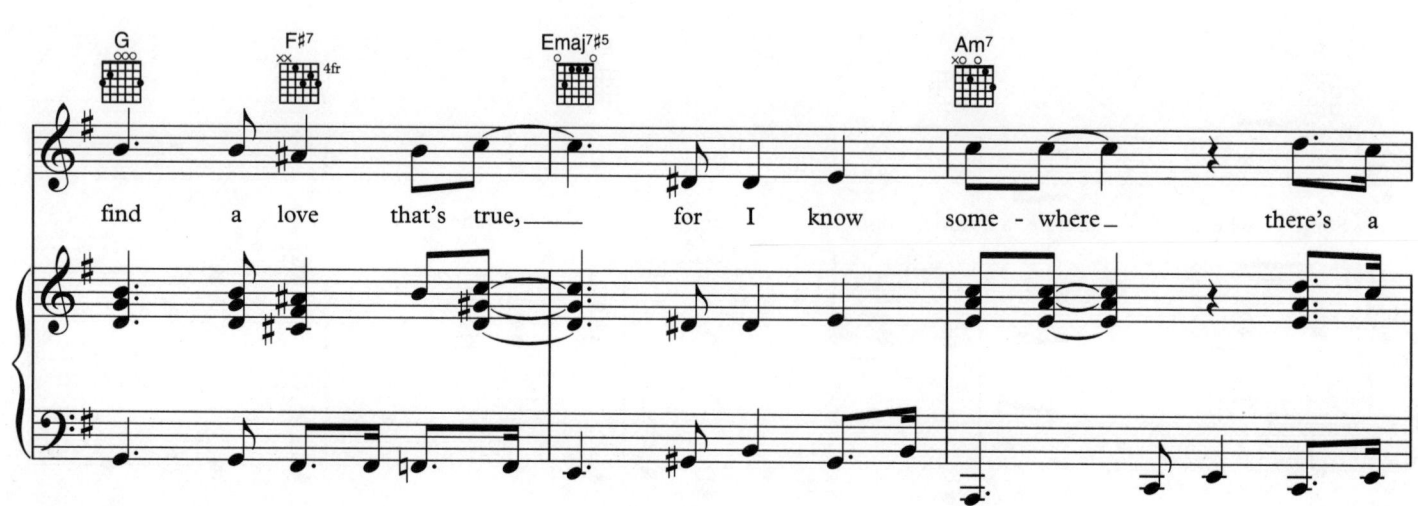

31

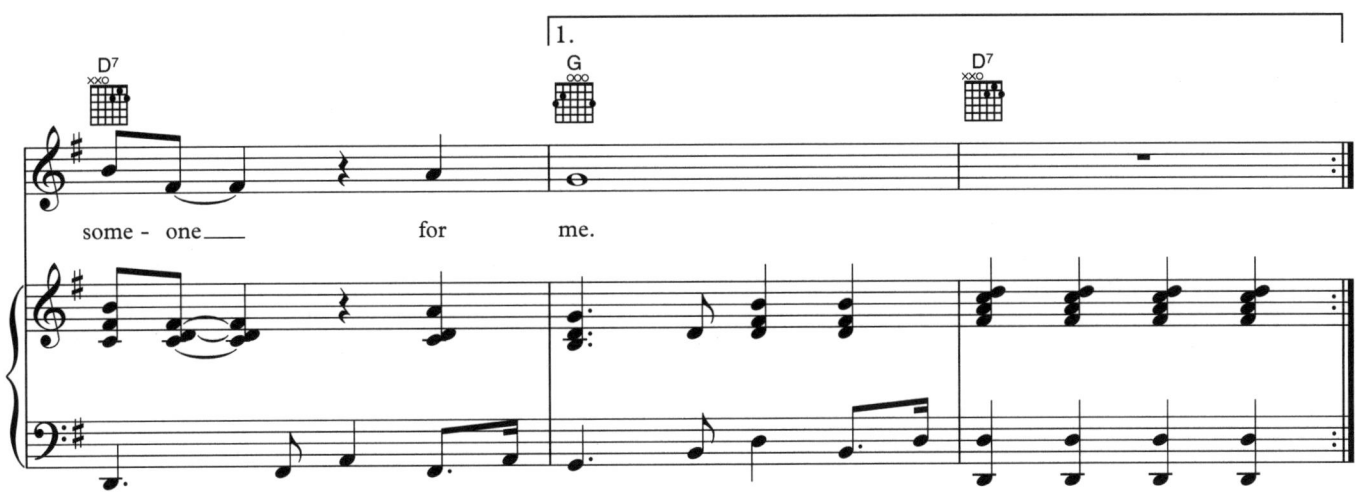
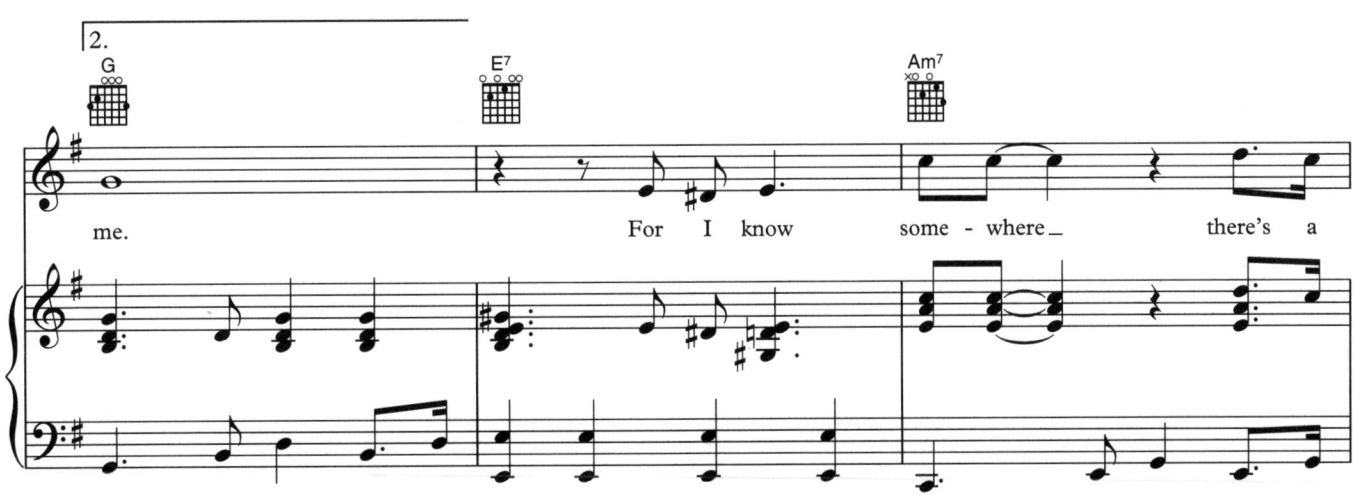
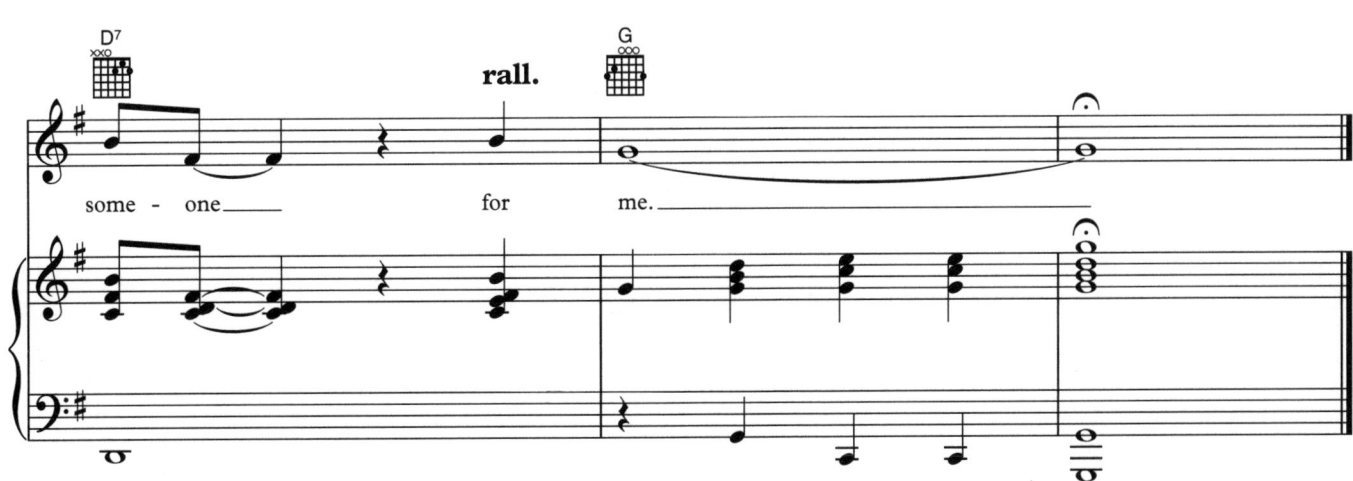

That's Amore

Track
8
Backing

Words by Jack Brooks
Music by Harry Warren

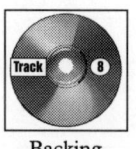

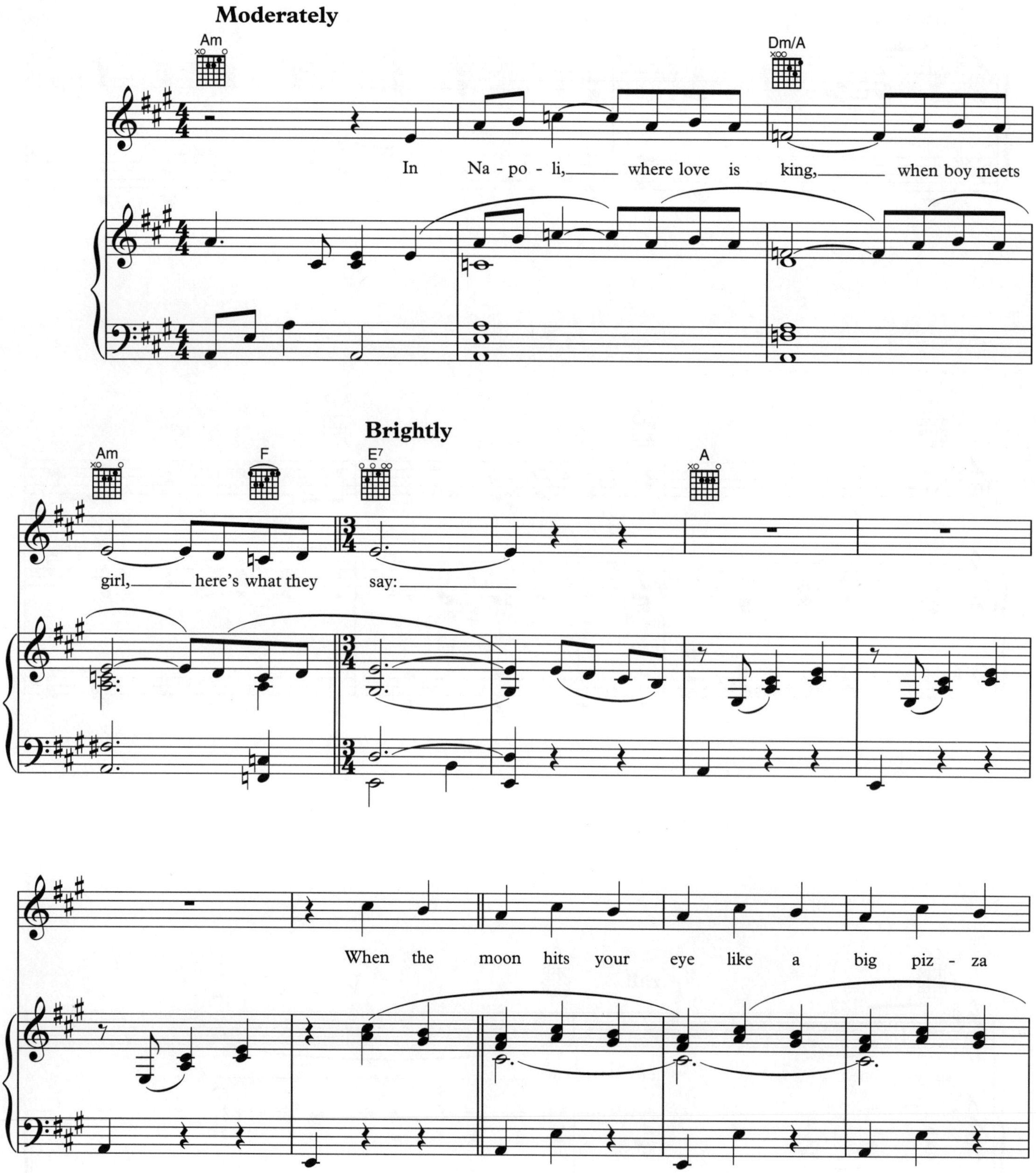
Moderately
Am
Dm/A
In Na - po - li, where love is king, when boy meets
Brightly
Am
F
E7
A
girl, here's what they say:
When the moon hits your eye like a big piz - za

© 1953 Paramount-Music Corp, Four-Jays-Music Co, USA and Peermusic (UK) Ltd
Famous Music Corp, London W1D 3JB and Peermusic (UK) Ltd, London WC1X 8LZ

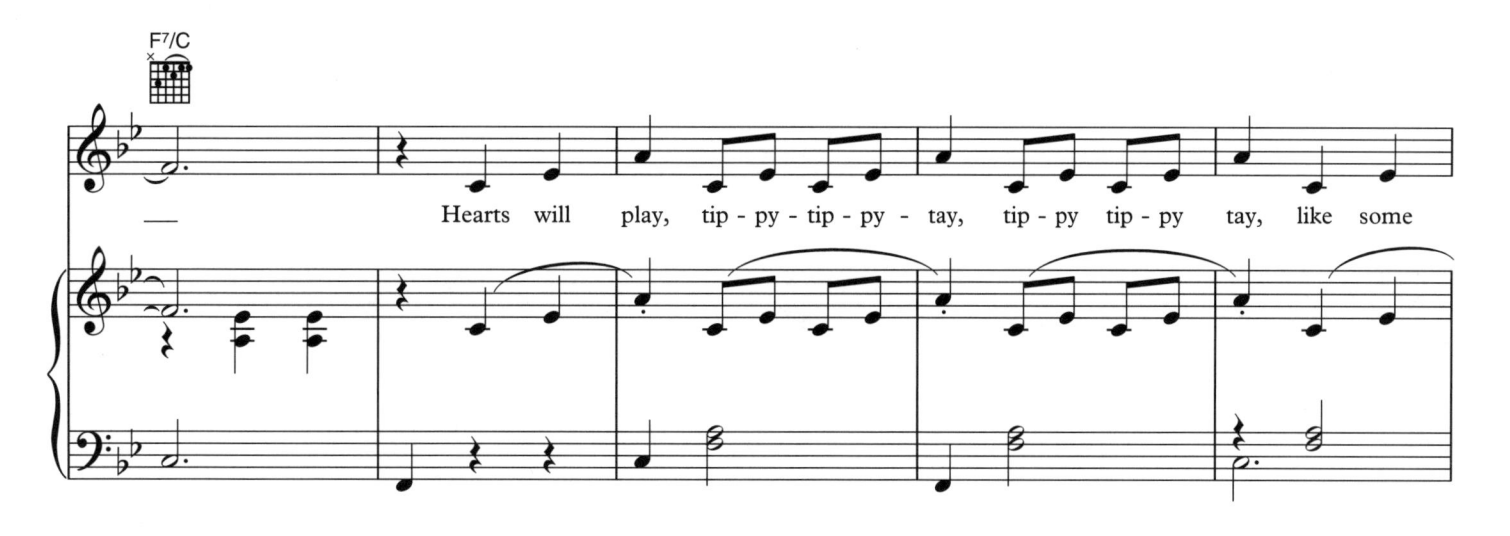

Hearts will play, tip-py-tip-py-tay, tip-py tip-py tay, like some gay ta-ran-tel-la. When the stars make you drool just like pas-ta fa-zool, that's a-mo-ré.

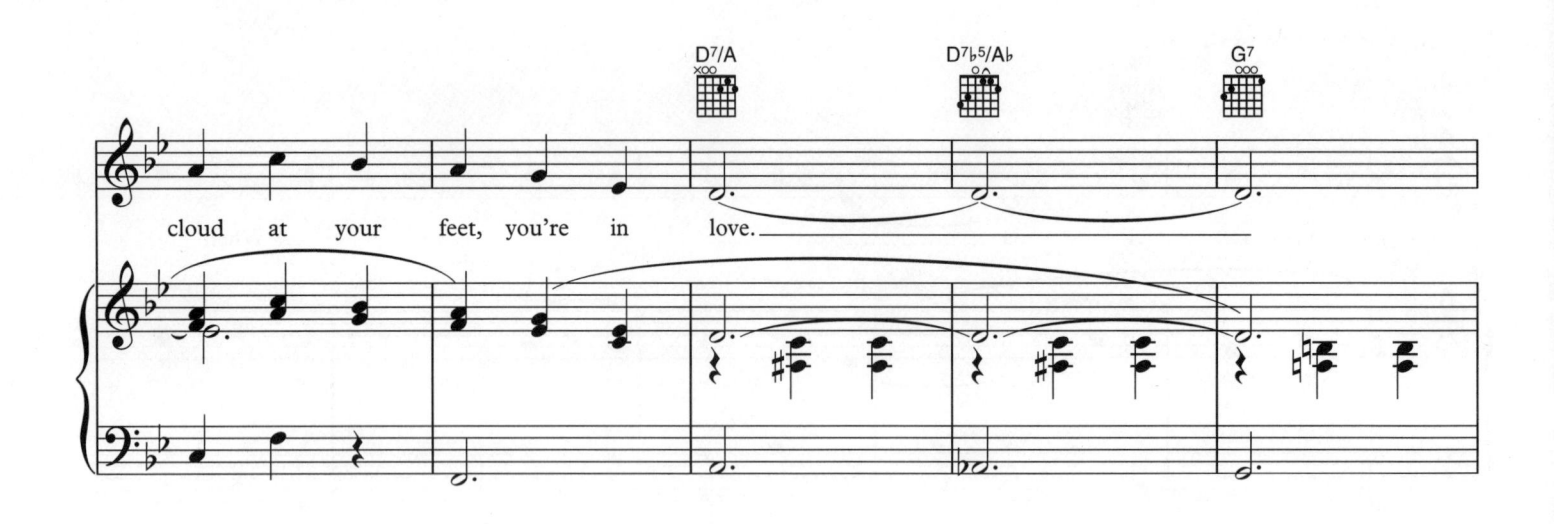

When you dance down the street with a cloud at your feet, you're in love. When you walk in a dream, but you know you're not dreaming, sig-

B♭
B♭maj7/A
Gm7
D♭dim7
F7/C
D♭dim7
no - - ré, scuz - za me, but you
F7/C
D♭dim7
F7
B♭
see, back in old Na - po - li, that's a - mo - ré, a -
G♭
F
B♭
mo - ré that's a - mo - ré.

Volare

English Words by Mitchell Parish
Music by Domenico Modugno

Moderato

Vo - la - re, oh, oh!
la - re, oh, oh!

Can - ta - re, oh, oh, oh, oh!
Can - ta - re, oh, oh, oh, oh!

Let's fly way up to the clouds, a - way from the mad - den - ing
Nel blu, di - pin - to di blu, fe - li - ce di sta - re las

© 1958 EMI Catalogue Partnership, EMI Robbins Catalog Inc, Edizioni Curzi and EMI United Partnership Ltd, USA
Worldwide print rights controlled by Warner Bros Publications Inc/IMP Ltd

A
F#m
F#m7
F#m6
13
crowds; We can sing in the glow of a star that I know of, where
sù. E vo - la - vo, vo - la - vo fe - li - ce più in al - to del
C#m
G#aug7
C#m7
C#7
Bm
16
lov - ers en - joy peace of mind, let us leave the con - fu - sion and
so - le ed an - co - ra più su, men - tre il mon - do pian pia - no spa -
C#7
F#m
D
F#m
19
all dis - il - lu - sion be - hind, just like
- ri - va lon - ta - no lag - giù, u - na

birds of a fea - ther a rain - bow to - ge - ther we'll find.
mu - si - ca dol - ce suo - na - va sol - tan - to per me.

Vo - la - re, oh, oh!
Vo - la - re, oh, oh!

Can - ta - re, oh, oh, oh, oh!
Can - ta - re, oh, oh, oh, oh!

No wonder my happy heart sings, your love has given me wings. *Pen - so che un so - gno co - sì non ri - tor - ni mai più*

mi di - pin - ge - ro le ma - ni e la fac - cia di blu,

poi d'im - prov - vi - so ve - ni - vo dal ven - to ra -

-pi - to e in - co - min - cia - vo a vo -

-la - re nel cie - lo in - fi - ni - to. _____ Vo -

2.
wings. Nel blu, di - pin - to di - blu, fe -

-li - ce di sta - re las sù. Nel di - pin - to di - blu.

Rio Bravo

Words by Paul Francis Webster
Music by Dimitri Tiomkin

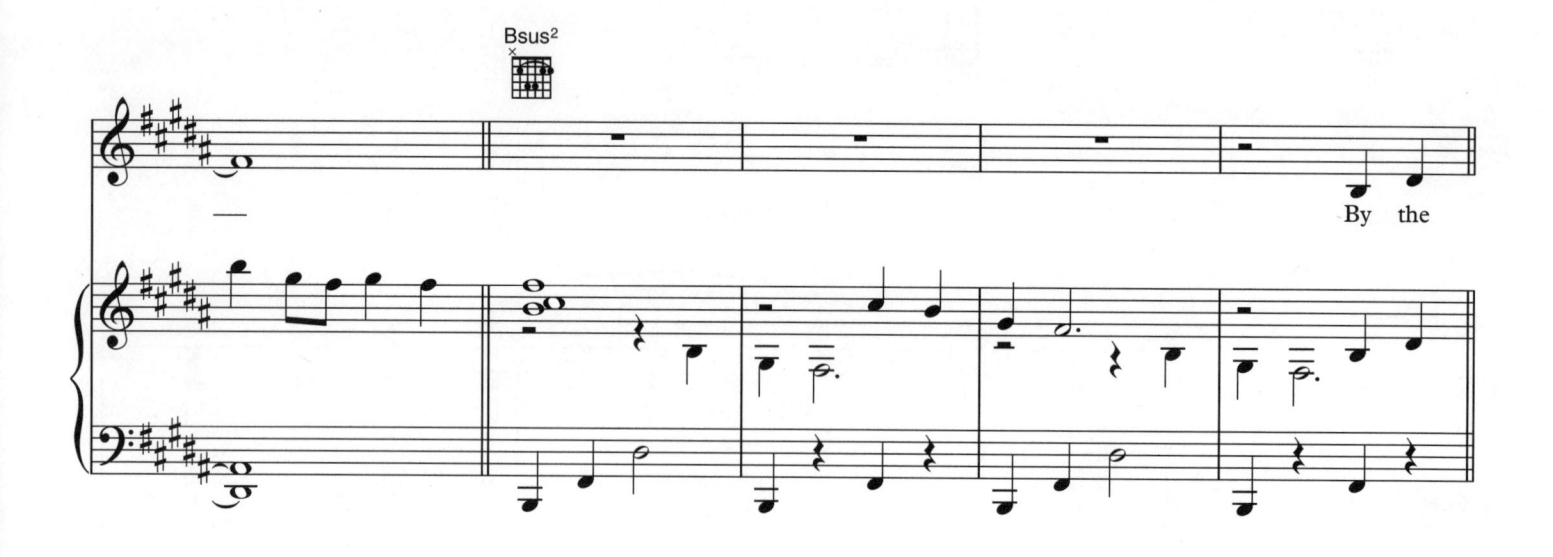

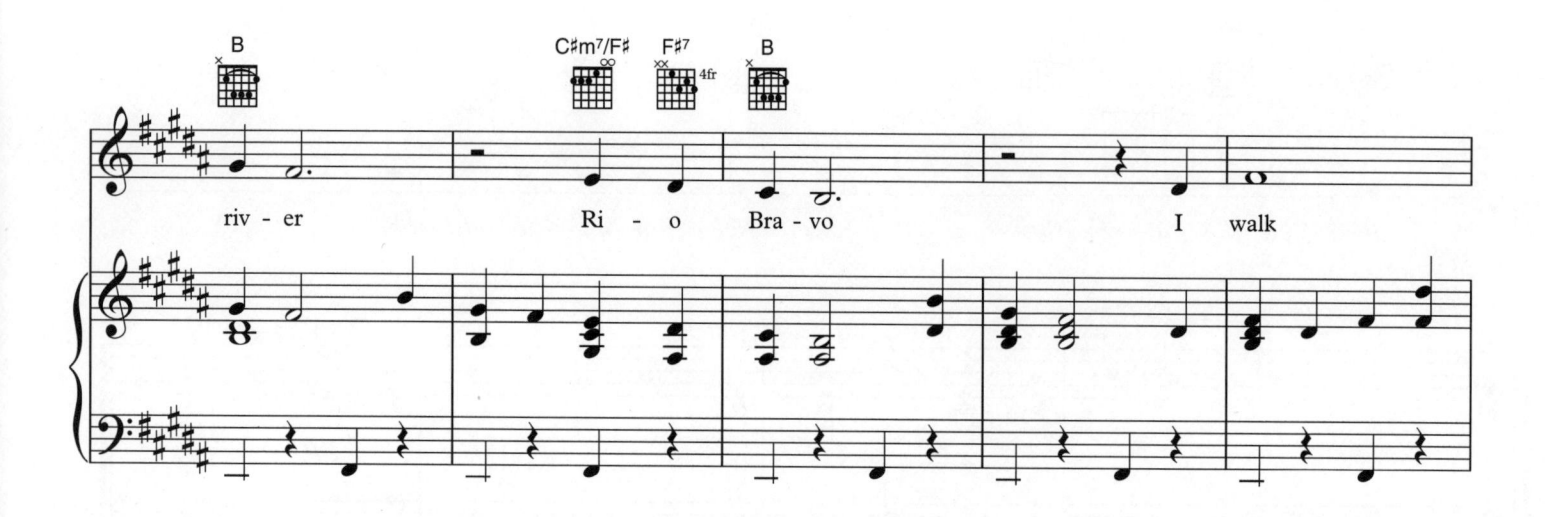

Moderately

Choir: Ri - o Bra - vo. By the riv - er Ri - o Bra - vo I walk

© 1959 M Witmark & Sons, USA
Warner/Chappell North America Ltd, London W6 8BS

all alone, and I wonder as I wander by the river where my love has flown. All the birds in the cotton woods above her know I love her,

know I care, but my dreams like the songs she sang in Spanish seem to vanish in the air, I wonder where. So I wonder as I wander will love come along?

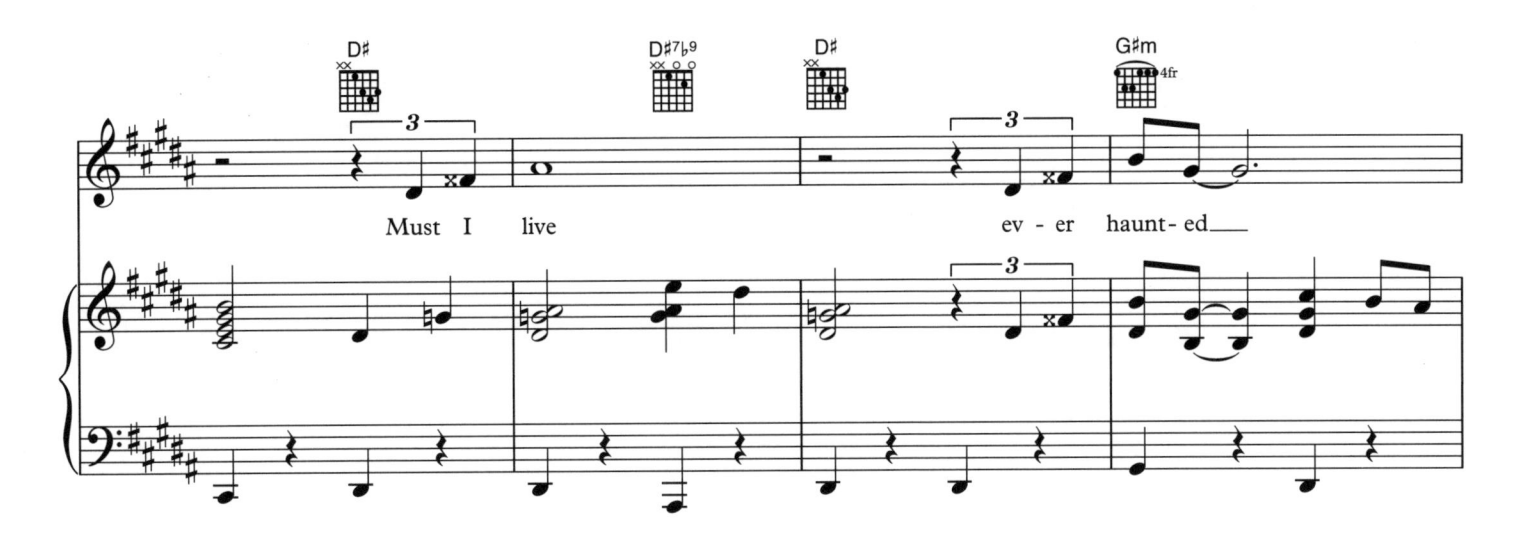

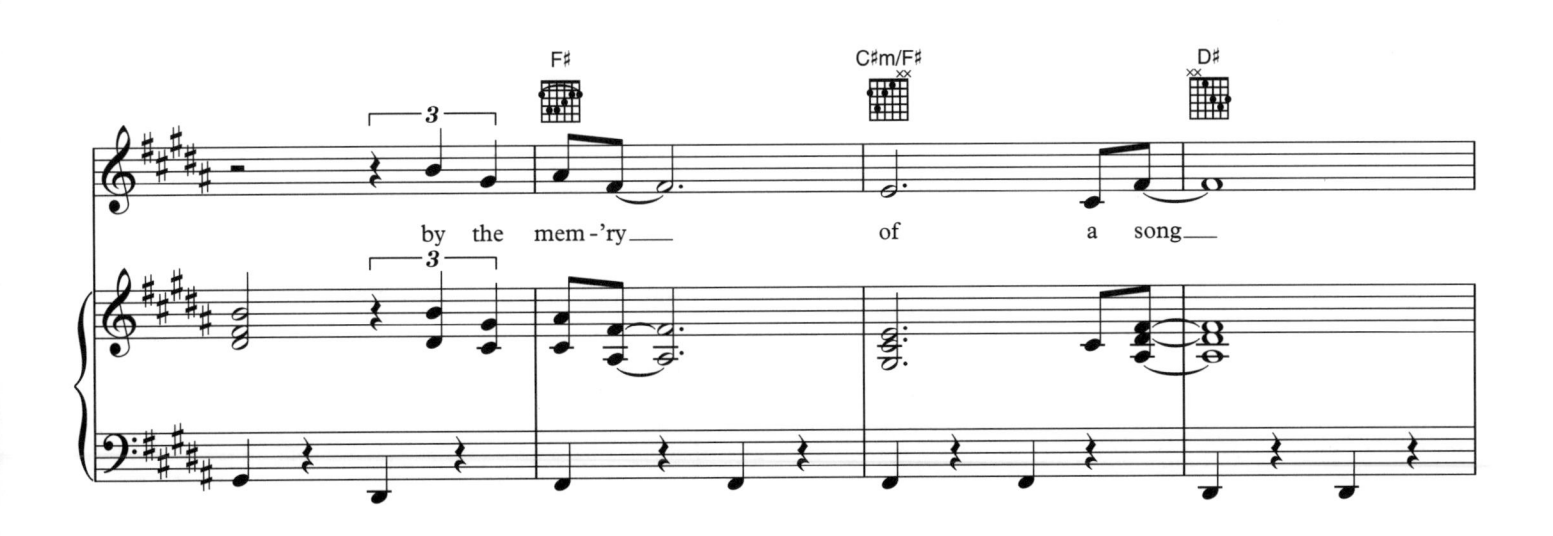

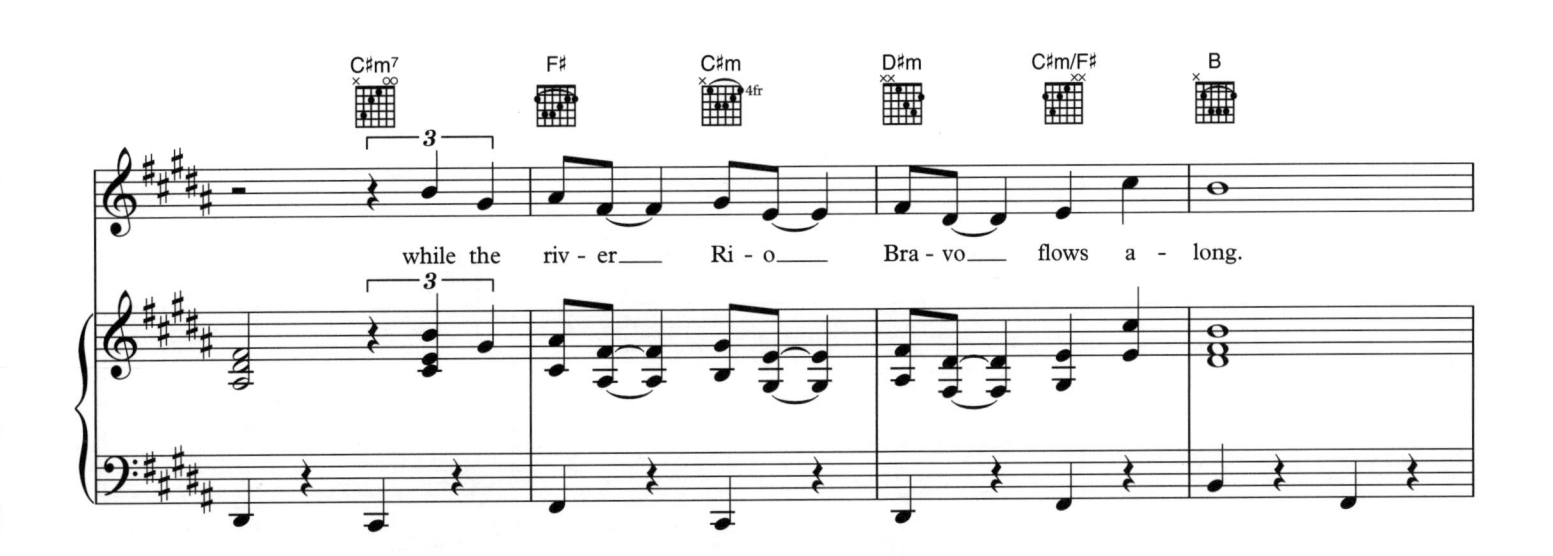

Must I live ev - er haunt - ed by the mem-'ry of a song while the riv - er Ri - o Bra - vo flows a - long.

Choir: Ri - o Bra - vo,___ Ri - o Bra - vo.___

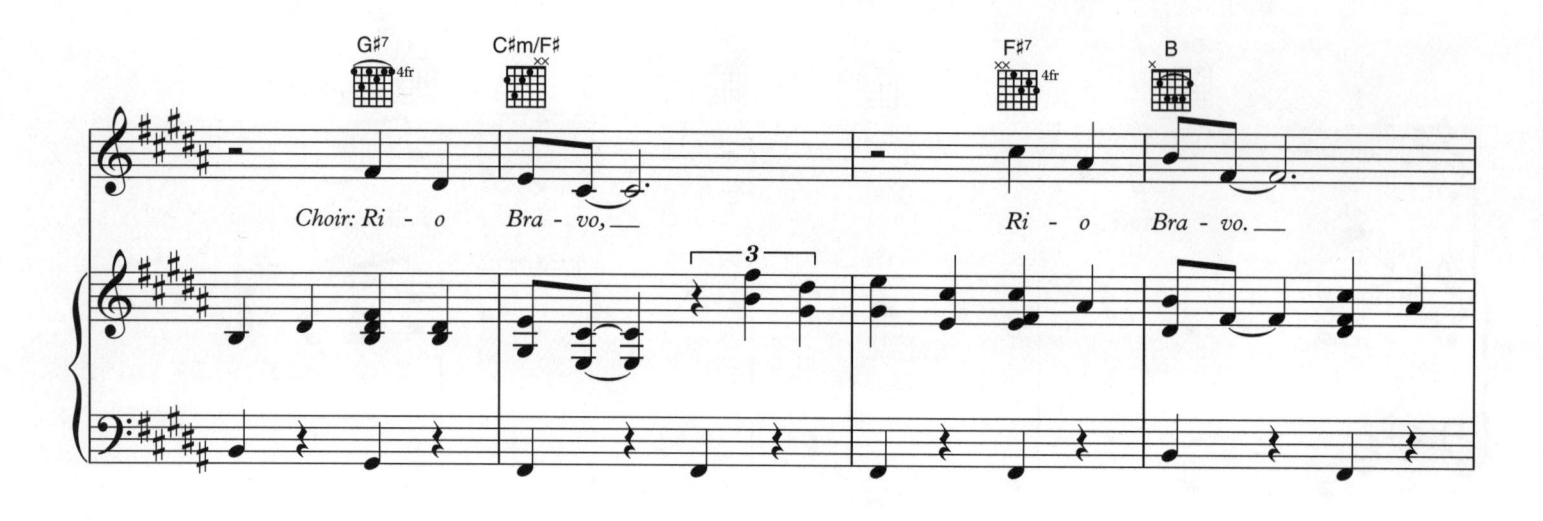

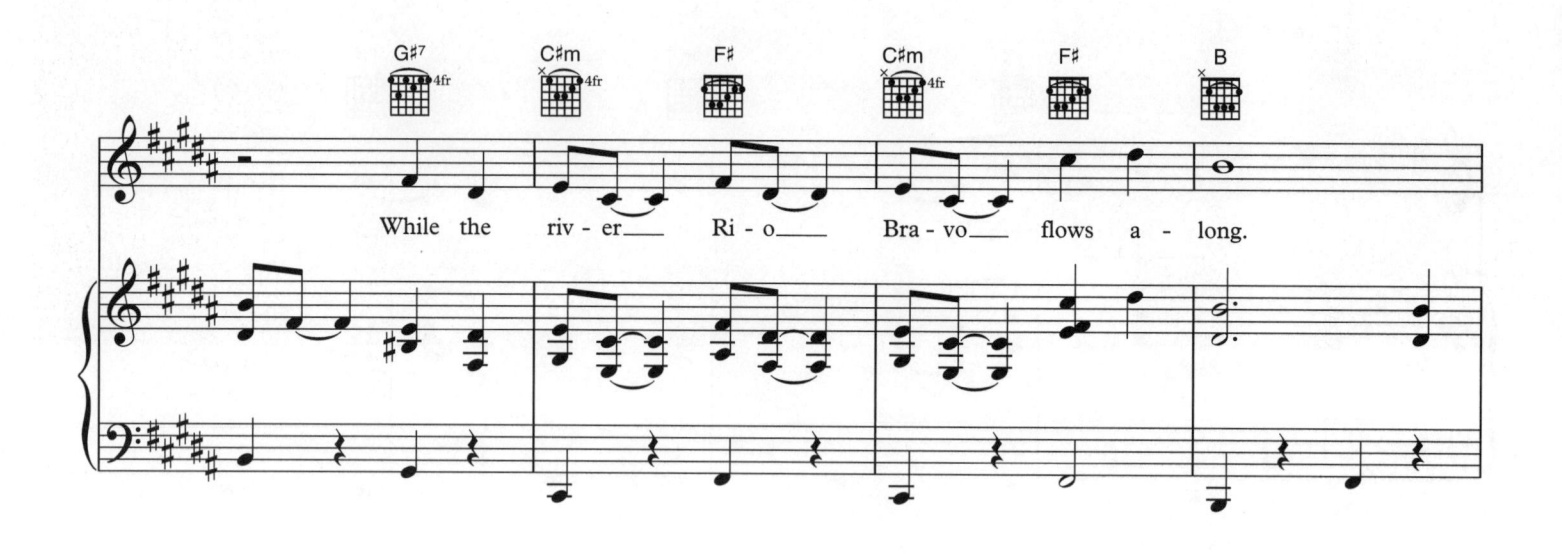

While the riv - er___ Ri - o___ Bra - vo___ flows a - long.

Choir: Ri - o Bra - vo.___

YOU'RE THE VOICE

Maria Callas — 8861A PV/CD
Casta Diva from Norma – Vissi D'arte from Tosca – Un Bel Di Vedremo from Madama Butterfly – Addio, Del Passato from La Traviata – J'ai Perdu Mon Eurydice from Orphee Et Eurydice – Les Tringles Des Sistres Tintaient from Carmen – Porgi Amor from Le Nozze Di Figaro – Ave Maria from Otello

Tom Jones — 8860A PVG/CD
Delilah – Green Green Grass Of Home – Help Yourself – I'll Never Fall In Love Again – It's Not Unusual – Mama Told Me Not To Come – Sexbomb – Thunderball – What's New Pussycat – You Can Leave Your Hat On

Celine Dion — 9297A PVG/CD
Beauty And The Beast – Because You Loved Me – Falling Into You – The First Time Ever I Saw Your Face – It's All Coming Back To Me Now – Misled – My Heart Will Go On – The Power Of Love – Think Twice – When I Fall In Love

Aretha Franklin — 9349A PVG/CD
Chain Of Fools – A Deeper Love Do Right Woman, Do Right Man – I Knew You Were Waiting (For Me) – I Never Loved A Man (The Way I Loved You) – I Say A Little Prayer – Respect – Think – Who's Zooming Who – (You Make Me Feel Like) A Natural Woman

George Michael — 9007A PVG/CD
Careless Whisper – A Different Corner – Faith – Father Figure – Freedom '90 – I'm Your Man – I Knew You Were Waiting (For Me) – Jesus To A Child – Older – Outside

Nina Simone — 9606A PVG/CD
Don't Let Me Be Misunderstood – Feeling Good – I Loves You Porgy – I Put A Spell On You – Love Me Or Leave Me – Mood Indigo – My Baby Just Cares For Me – Ne Me Quitte Pas (If You Go Away) – Nobody Knows You When You're Down And Out – Take Me To The Water

Carole King — 9700A PVG/CD
Beautiful – Crying In The Rain – I Feel The Earth Move – It's Too Late – (You Make Me Feel Like) A Natural Woman – So Far Away – Way Over Yonder – Where You Lead – Will You Love Me Tomorrow – You've Got A Friend

Frank Sinatra — 9746A PVG/CD
April In Paris – Come Rain Or Come Shine – Fly Me To The Moon (In Other Words) – I've Got You Under My Skin – The Lady Is A Tramp – My Kinda Town (Chicago Is) – My Way – Theme From *New York, New York* – Someone To Watch Over Me – Something Stupid

Barbra Streisand — 9770A PVG/CD
Cry Me A River – Evergreen (A Star Is Born) – Happy Days Are Here Again – I've Dreamed Of You – Memory – My Heart Belongs To Me – On A Clear Day (You Can See Forever) – Someday My Prince Will Come – Tell Him (duet with Celine Dion) – The Way We Were

Bette Midler — 9799A PVG/CD
Boogie Woogie Bugle Boy – Chapel Of Love – Friends – From A Distance – Hello In There – One For My Baby (And One More For The Road) – Only In Miami – The Rose – When A Man Loves A Woman – Wind Beneath My Wings

Eva Cassidy — 9810A PVG/CD
Ain't No Sunshine – Autumn Leaves – How Can I Keep From Singing – Imagine – It Doesn't Matter Anymore – Over The Rainbow – Penny To My Name – People Get Ready – Wayfaring Stranger – What A Wonderful World

Matt Monro — 9889A PVG/CD
Around The World – Born Free – From Russia With Love – Gonna Build A Mountain – The Impossible Dream – My Kind Of Girl – On A Clear Day You Can See Forever – Portrait Of My Love – Softly As I Leave You – Walk Away

Billie Holiday — 10039A PVG/CD
All Of Me – Body And Soul – God Bless The Child – I Love My Man ('Billie's Blues') – Lady Sings The Blues – Lover Man (Oh Where Can You Be) – The Man I Love – My Man ('Mon Homme') – Night And Day – St. Louis Blues

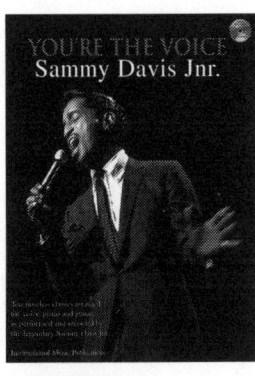

Sammy Davis Jnr. — 10091A PVG/CD
For Once In My Life – Hey There – It's All Right With Me – I've Gotta Be Me – Let's Face The Music And Dance – Love Me Or Leave Me – Mr Bojangles – September Song – Something's Gotta Give – What Kind Of Fool Am I?

Norah Jones — 10119A PVG/CD
Come Away With Me – Don't Know Why – Don't Miss You At All – Feelin' The Same Way – Nightingale – Painter Song – The Prettiest Thing – Sunrise – Those Sweet Words – What Am I To You?

The outstanding vocal series from IMP

CD contains full backings for each song, professionally arranged to recreate the sounds of the original recording

Essential Audition Songs

Broadway (Female)
7171A Book and CD

Broadway (Male)
9185A Book and CD

Pop Ballads (Female)
6939A Book and CD

Pop Ballads (Male)
9776A Book and CD

Pop Divas
7769A Book and CD

Kids
7341A Book and CD

Jazz Standards
7021A Book and CD

Timeless Crooners
9495A Book and CD

Duets
7432A Book and CD

Movie Hits
9186A Book and CD

Wannabe Pop Stars
9735A Book and CD

Love Songs
9841A Book and CD

Big Band Hits
9725A Book and CD

West End Hits
10009A Book and CD